The Old Synagogue

To my father,
Archie Rosenblum

*The publication of this book was made
possible by a gift in memory of
Harry Elson*

Text and illustrations copyright © 1989 by Richard Rosenblum
Design by Edith T. Weinberg
All rights reserved.
First edition.
Manufactured in the United States of America

10   9   8   7   6   5   4   3   2

Library of Congress Cataloging-in-Publication Data

Rosenblum, Richard.
    The old synagogue / by Richard Rosenblum.
        p.   cm.
    Summary: A once-beautiful synagogue on a crowded street in a big
city is abandoned and becomes a factory when the original
neighborhood inhabitants become more prosperous and move away; but
as time goes by young Jewish families rediscover the area, move in,
and restore to beauty the old synagogue.
    ISBN 0-8276-0322-3
    1. Synagogues—United States—Juvenile literature.
[1. Synagogues.   2. City and town life.]   I. Title.
BM653.R59 1989
296.6'5—dc 19   89-1884
                                                            CIP
                                                            AC

The Old Synagogue

by Richard Rosenblum

AN EDWARD E. ELSON BOOK

THE JEWISH PUBLICATION SOCIETY

Philadelphia—New York

5749—1989

Back in the time of your great-grandparents, some Jewish people came to America, together with their rabbi, from the same little village in Europe. They decided to have a synagogue of their own.

They built it on a street near where they all lived. It was a crowded street, full of stores. There was a kosher butcher and a bakery with bagels and large loaves of black bread. There was a delicatessen and a store that sold appetizers, salty lox, herring, and sour pickles.

Large families lived in small apartments above the stores. These people were poor.

Many of them attended the synagogue. They came for morning and evening services. They came, wearing their best clothes, for the Sabbath and for holidays. They were happy at bar mitzvahs and weddings, and sad at funerals.

Everyone loved the synagogue. It was small but elegant.

There were stained-glass windows in the front and back of the synagogue. The window over the entrance door had a Jewish star.

In the front of the synagogue was an Ark. It was a carved wooden cabinet that held three Torah scrolls. An embroidered curtain covered the front of the Ark.

In the middle of the room there was the bimah, a platform with a

wooden railing around it. On the bimah was a table covered with a red-velvet cloth.

On the Sabbath, holidays, Mondays, and Thursdays, members of the congregation took one or more of the Torahs from the Ark, placed them on the table, and read from them.

The men in this Orthodox synagogue sat on benches around three sides of the bimah, and the women sat in the balcony, above.

As time passed, people became more prosperous. Their sons and
daughters grew up and began to move away.

Fewer and fewer members of the congregation remained in the old neighborhood. The ones who stayed were mostly the older people. Very few Jewish people moved in to replace those who left. Often, there were not the ten men for a minyan, the group required to hold a service, read the Torah, or recite certain prayers.

The few men who were left decided to close the old synagogue and sell the building. They sold it to a man who turned it into a small factory. The members of the old synagogue gave the money to a synagogue in Israel.

The bimah and the Ark were sold, but the stained-glass windows remained. Mr. Rosenfeld, whose grandfather had helped organize the synagogue, stayed in the neighborhood. He wrapped each Torah in a tallit and took it home. He put the Torahs in a glass bookcase in his living room. He also kept some of the prayerbooks and Bibles. The worn-out and torn ones he buried.

Mr. Rosenfeld formed a minyan from among the few Jewish men
left in the area, and for many years they held services in his living room.

The stores on the street changed. The butcher shop was no longer
kosher, the herring and lox store closed, and the baker moved to Florida.
Some stores were boarded up.

It was a very sad time for the synagogue and for the street. It remained that way for many years. But just when the street looked its worst, it started to change again.

People who couldn't find other places to live in the big, crowded city discovered this old neighborhood. They slowly moved in and fixed up the old buildings. Some Jewish families began to think that it would be nice to have a little synagogue of their own in the neighborhood. They noticed the old building with the stained-glass windows and the Jewish star.

They looked inside and found a big room filled with people at sewing machines making blouses. Despite a few holes and cracks, the stained-glass windows and the old balcony were in good condition.

They decided to organize a congregation and hire a young rabbi. Together they raised enough money to buy the old building so that they could turn it into a synagogue once again.

They hired carpenters, painters, and electricians to fix up the building, repair the balcony, and mend the stained-glass windows. There was a kibbutz in Israel that made synagogue furniture. From it they ordered a new bimah, an Ark, and wooden benches.

One day Mr. Rosenfeld appeared. He said he lived around the corner and had the Torahs from the old synagogue in his apartment. The new congregation was overjoyed to hear the news.

They bought new silver crowns and breastplates for the old Torahs. Members of the congregation made gifts of new prayerbooks and Bibles. Someone promised an Eternal Light. Others got together and embroidered new curtains for the Ark and a coverlet with Jewish decorations for the table on the bimah.

Members of the congregation were busy. They installed the new furniture from Israel. They put the new curtains and the table coverlet in their places. The synagogue looked as beautiful as it did when it first opened many, many years ago.

Now it was time to dedicate the synagogue.

On a Sunday morning just before Rosh Hashanah, the Jewish New Year, the congregation held a parade. It started in front of Mr. Rosenfeld's house. Mr. Rosenfeld, the rabbi, and the president of the

congregation each carried a Torah. A man blowing a shofar and people
waving flags followed. Then came a group of musicians who played
traditional Jewish songs and dances. The whole congregation marched
behind the band. The Torahs were coming home!

Many people came to the ceremony. A congressman, a city councilmember, and ministers from nearby churches were there. They welcomed the old synagogue with its new congregation to the neighborhood. The Torahs were placed in the new Ark, and the rabbi quoted from the Bible, "Out of Zion shall come forth the Torah."

When the ceremony was over, the happy congregation and its guests went downstairs to the new community center in the basement and had a big party. The band played while people sang and danced the hora. Tables were covered with platters of wonderful food—lox and other smoked fish, cheeses, all kinds of salads, rolls, bagels, and black bread, and big cakes, and piles of cookies.

The people danced and sang all day.

A few days later, the congregation returned to their new old synagogue and celebrated the New Year together.